Career Pathways in Cyber Security: From Classroom to Boardroom

Professor Edward Moskal

Copyright © 2024 Edward Moskal

All rights reserved.

ISBN: 9798320112732

DEDICATION

This book is dedicated to the Saint Peter's University faculty and administration that I have worked with and been associated with during my career. Also, to iQ4 Corporation, for its work to solve the cyber security skills gap, using artificial intelligence and machine learning to develop-out a next-generation "Digital Achievement Wallet".

CONTENTS

Acknowledgments

1.	The Cyber Security Job Shortage	3
2.	Closing the Skill Gap	6
3.	Credentials and Certifications	9
4.	Hiring Trend: Degrees vs Skills	16
5.	Internships and Apprenticeships	21
6.	Digital Achievement Wallet	24
7.	How to Land the Job	35
8.	Working with Others	41
9.	References	45

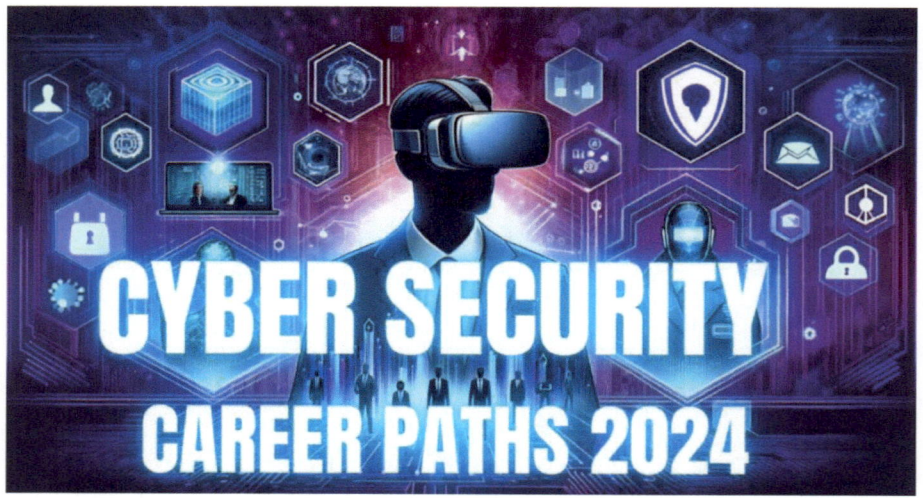

ACKNOWLEDGMENTS

This book is based on my knowledge and information acquired from working in industry, teaching at the college level, and research focusing on closing the cyber security skills gap.

1. THE CYBER SECURITY JOB SHORTAGE

As our global society embraces more complex and innovative ways of using technology, criminals are using that same technology maliciously. The threat is so urgent, and the need for cyber workers is so critical, that the White House established the National Cyber Workforce and Education Strategy (NCWES) to address both the immediate and long-term cybersecurity workforce needs. Just as there was, and still is, a shortage of healthcare workers, there are not enough cyber professionals on the front lines. Worldwide, the cybersecurity workforce shortfall will likely be approximately 3.5 million people by 2025, according to Cybersecurity Ventures. In the United States, according to CyberSeek there are 572,392 cyber security job vacancies as of this publication.

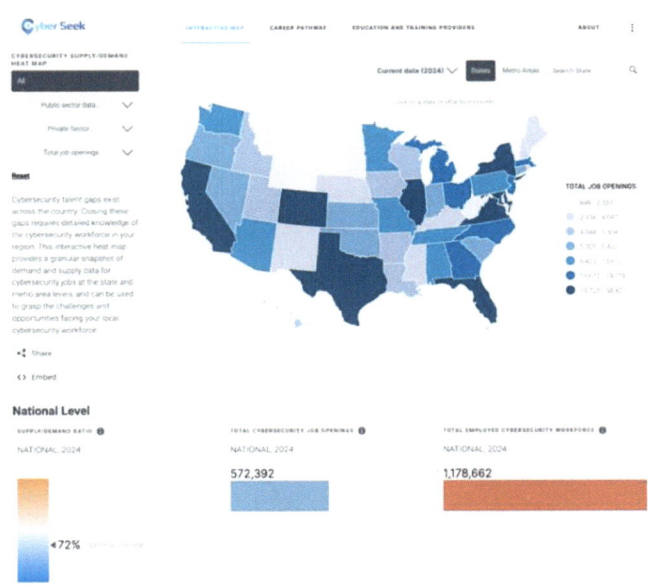

Because the demand for cybersecurity professionals has increased so much, it is making the job market highly competitive. To reduce the number of applicants and identify more candidates that fit the job role, some employers may be using experience requirements as a filter.

Many factors have come together to cause the cybersecurity skills gap. Here are five top causes:

1. The demand for cybersecurity talent keeps increasing: Not only has nearly every organization become completely dependent on technology, but technology also continues to become more complex. Securing today's systems, networks and data against cyber-attacks is tougher than ever, with even more security technologies and processes needed to work in concert with each other. So, organizations need their cyber workforces to be larger and have a wider range of skills than ever before.
2. The pool of cybersecurity talent lacks diversity: According to a recent workforce study from ISC2, only about 25% of the cybersecurity workforce around the world is female. Another ISC2 study indicated that, although cybersecurity teams are becoming increasingly diverse, this is happening slowly. According to the research, 70% of cybersecurity workers 60 and older are white men, 13% are white women, 15% are non-white men and 2% are non-white women.
3. Employers have unrealistic expectations: Cybersecurity job descriptions often require college degrees, multiple certifications and years and years of experience in a variety of security disciplines. Many candidates who would be assets to organizations don't apply for these jobs because they assume that the requirements are truly required. Others do apply but don't even get a call back because they lack a degree or sufficient hands-on experience.
4. Employees aren't keeping their skills up to date: The challenges that employers need to tackle change over time, such as the increasing reliance on cloud security and the evolving threats against data and systems. Employees are so overworked that they often don't have the opportunity to learn new skills, attend training, take online courses or pursue new certifications. And this isn't just technical skills, soft skills like communication are writing are also needed.
5. Cybersecurity experts are leaving the profession: Alarmingly, a recent survey commissioned by Trellix found that over one-third of the cybersecurity workforce are planning to change careers. There's a major employee retention problem, due in large part to constant staffing shortages and the incredible pressure of many cybersecurity jobs.

Cybersecurity Skills Gap: Why it Exists and How to Fix it

To tackle the cybersecurity job shortage, businesses are focusing on:

- investing in training
- upskilling and reskilling their current workforce
- diversity, equity, and inclusion (DEI) initiatives
- providing more flexible working conditions
- alternative recruiting methods, and
- using technology to automate aspects of cybersecurity.

As the world continues to move more heavily into digital, the value of cybersecurity staffing cannot be overstated. Businesses are increasingly investing in comprehensive digital protection, placing cybersecurity at the forefront of their strategy. As such, the demand for qualified professionals in the field is rising at an unprecedented rate.

2. CLOSING THE SKILL GAP

The cybersecurity skill gap presents a threat to information systems security best practices and can lead to businesses facing cybersecurity workforce burnout. In addition, the skills shortage impacts cybersecurity industry functionality, vulnerability, and penetration testing, affecting cybersecurity talent management and services. The consequences of the cybersecurity skills gap are evident in the strain on businesses' security infrastructure and operations.

A recent survey by RSM (a consulting firm providing audit, tax, and consulting services focused on the middle market) found out that:

- Hiring is a challenge for nearly all middle market companies, and needed skills are in short supply.
- Existing workers are being burned out, creating a vicious cycle of employee turnover.
- Companies are being hardest hit in their most critical areas.
- Outsourcing/managed services can solve talent gaps and other middle market pain points.

In addressing the cybersecurity skills gap, organizations can improve cybersecurity posture and resilience through upskilling and reskilling their workforce, recruiting, and training a diverse workforce and creating a holistic cybersecurity ecosystem. With a cybersecurity workforce gap of 3.5 million people, businesses can't rely on filling open positions only with "traditional" candidates, those with four-year cybersecurity degrees, or individuals with related work experience.

Here are several ways the cybersecurity skills gap can shrink.

Offer Ongoing Training Opportunities for Existing Security Professionals

As organizations of all sizes struggle to recruit qualified security professionals, leaders inevitably worry about retaining the personnel they already have on staff. Offering team members opportunities to pursue advanced training and certification programs not only keeps their skills sharp but is a great way to enhance employee experience and job satisfaction. According to a study conducted by the Society of Human Resource Management (SHRM) Research Institute, 86% of human resources managers surveyed say that offering ongoing training helps with staff retention.

There are numerous high-quality cybersecurity training and certification programs available. Some examples include CompTIA, EC-Council, ISC2, ISACA, and SANS Institute. These organizations offer a variety of both self-paced and instructor-led training and multi-level certification programs for learners of all skill levels. Programs like these give participants the security, networking, and information technology knowledge needed to help them progress in any role and at any point in their career. For those just getting started in the industry, these programs offer strong foundational knowledge to set learners up for future success.

Recruit Talent from Untapped Communities

Attracting new talent to the field is an essential component of addressing the skills shortage, and offering accessible cyber training is a great way to recruit professionals looking for a career change. Transitioning military and veterans are a great example of a talent pool that can be a tremendous asset to the cybersecurity industry. Recognizing that those in the military community have many transferrable skills, such as leadership, communication, and attention to detail, to name a few. Military and veterans are by nature problem-solvers who understand the importance of maintaining a strong defense posture and following the chain of command when dealing with an active threat. There are military/veteran national organizations like Hiring Our Heroes and State led programs like INVETS that work with military/veterans to help close the cybersecurity skills gap by helping facilitate the transition of military service members, veterans, and military spouses into the cybersecurity industry.

Additionally, women make up only 24% of today's cybersecurity workforce. Yet a wealth of data illustrates the many benefits of building diverse teams. For women looking to jump-start a career in cybersecurity, or for those who work in the technology sector already but are interested in exploring security-focused roles, numerous resources are available to support that transition. Organizations like WiCyS provide members access to industry-leading training and certification curriculum, networking and mentoring programs, internships, and full-time employment opportunities. And the SANS Institute offers several education programs for women interested in pursuing cybersecurity roles, such as the accelerated Women's Immersion Academy program and the New2Cyber curriculum that teaches foundational cyber skills.

Partner with and Recruit from Higher Education Institutions

As cyberattacks grow in volume and sophistication and the skills shortage continues to strain security teams, many colleges and universities are dedicating more resources to creating or expanding cybersecurity-focused degree programs. Today, almost 400 higher education institutions have earned the "National Centers of Academic Excellence in Cybersecurity" designation from the National Security Agency, a stark contrast compared to the 12 schools that had achieved this as of 2010.

Public and private sector organizations have a role to play here as well and must partner with educational institutions to collectively build the future cybersecurity workforce. For example, the Fortinet Academic Partner Program works with over 500 colleges and universities globally to integrate the award-winning Fortinet Network Security Expert (NSE) training and certification courses into the existing curriculum. Initiatives like this help set students up for success by giving them the opportunity to earn industry-recognized certifications before they even begin searching for employment.

Shrinking the Skills Gap Requires Thinking Outside the Box

The competition among organizations for qualified professionals will grow even fiercer. We can work to shrink this skills gap in a variety of ways, from implementing initiatives to helping retain existing team members, like offering ongoing professional development opportunities, to broadening the talent pools that are recruited.

If companies are to address the cybersecurity skill gap they should shift the balance of their security spending from security systems to people, processes, and alternative hiring practices, thus also reducing their risk exposure to staff leaving the company.

3. CREDENTIALS AND CERTIFICATIONS

While most cybersecurity professionals have at least a bachelor's degree in computer science/cybersecurity, many companies prefer candidates who also have a certification to validate knowledge and skills of best practices. There are hundreds of certifications available, from general to vendor-specific, entry-level to advanced. Before you spend your money and time on a certification, it's important to find one that will give you a competitive advantage in your career.

The table below identifies the number of U.S. job listings across three job sites (Linkedin, Indeed, Simply Hired) that require cybersecurity certification for popular certifications. The Security+ leads the way with 571,335 job listings.

Certification	LinkedIn	Indeed	Simply Hired	Total
CISSP	34,343	6,976	7,512	48,831
CISA	7,778	2,851	3,085	13,714
Security+	7,366	546,990	16,979	571,335
CEH	9,805	1,300	1,205	12,310
CISM	4,676	1,825	2,248	8,749
GSEC	3,342	1,720	1,743	6,805
SSCP	3,495	3,013	1,799	8,307
CASP	2,026	911	921	3,858
GCIH	1,957	991	1,078	4,026
OSCP	2,194	552	565	3,311

Number of US job search results for each certification as of September 2023

If you're just starting out in cybersecurity, consider an entry-level credential, like the Google Cybersecurity Professional Certificate. You can build job-ready skills while earning a shareable certificate from an industry leader.

Below is detail on the certifications listed in the above table.

Certified Information Systems Security Professional (CISSP)

The CISSP certification from the cybersecurity professional organization (ISC)² ranks among the most sought-after credential in the industry. Earning your CISSP demonstrates that you're experienced in IT security and capable of designing, implementing, and monitoring a cybersecurity program.

This advanced certification is for experienced security professionals looking to advance their careers in roles like:
- Chief information security officer - $193,081
- Security administrator - $62,869
- Security engineer - $108,705
- Senior security consultant - $133,113
- Information assurance analyst - $85,662

Requirements: To qualify to take the CISSP exam, you'll need five or more years of cumulative work experience in at least two of eight cybersecurity domains. These include Security and Risk Management, Asset Security, Security Architecture and Engineering, Communication and Network Security, Identity and Access Management, Security Assessment and Testing, Security Operations, and Software Development Security. A four-year degree in computer science satisfies one year of the work requirement. Part-time work and paid internships also count.
Cost (US): $749

Certified Information Systems Auditor (CISA)

This credential from IT professional association ISACA helps demonstrate your expertise in assessing security vulnerabilities, designing and implementing controls, and reporting on compliance. It's among the most recognized certifications for careers in cybersecurity auditing.

The CISA is designed for mid-level IT professionals looking to advance into jobs like:
- IT audit manager - $131,967
- Cybersecurity auditor - $81,452
- Information security analyst - $91,805
- IT security engineer - $108,705
- IT project manager - $105,332
- Compliance program manager - $102,314

Requirements: You need at least five years of experience in IT or IS audit, control, security, or assurance. A two or four-year degree can be substituted for one or two years of experience, respectively.
Cost: $575 for members, $760 for non-members

Certified Information Security Manager (CISM)

With the CISM certification, also from ISACA, you can validate your expertise in the management side of information security, including topics like governance, program development, and program, incident, and risk management.

If you're looking to pivot from the technical to the managerial side of cybersecurity, earning your CISM could be a good choice. Jobs that use the CISM include:
- IT manager - $111,347
- Information systems security officer - $96,884
- Information risk consultant - $92,795
- Director of information security - $149,835
- Data governance manager - $123,803

Requirements: To take the CISM exam, you need at least five years of experience in information security management. Satisfy up to two years of this requirement with general information security experience. You can also waive one or two years with another certification in good standing or a graduate degree in an information security-related field.
Cost: $575 for members, $760 for non-members

CompTIA Security+

CompTIA Security+ is an entry-level security certification that validates the core skills needed in any cybersecurity role. With this certification, you can demonstrate your ability to assess the security of an organization, monitor and secure cloud, mobile, and internet of things (IoT) environments, understand laws and regulations related to risk and compliance, and identify and respond to security incidents.

Earning your Security+ certification can help you in roles such as:
- Systems administrator - $78,402
- Help desk manager - $82,295
- Security engineer - $106,141
- Cloud engineer - $105,252
- Security administrator - $62,869
- IT auditor - $78,933

Requirements: While there are no strict requirements for taking the Security+ exam, you're encouraged to earn your Network+ certification first and gain at least two years of IT experience with a security focus.
Cost: $392

Certified Ethical Hacker (CEH)

Ethical hacking, also known as white hat hacking, penetration testing, or red team, involves lawfully hacking organizations to try and uncover vulnerabilities before malicious players do. The EC-Council offers the CEH Certified Ethical Hacker certification. Earn it to demonstrate your skills in penetration testing, attack detection, vectors, and prevention.

The CEH certification helps you to think like a hacker and take a more proactive approach to cybersecurity. Consider this certification for jobs like:
- Penetration tester - $93,973
- Cyber incident analyst - $62,445
- Threat intelligence analyst - $100,564
- Cloud security architect - $136,647
- Cybersecurity engineer - $99,382

Requirements: You can take the CEH exam if you have two years of work experience in information security or if you complete an official EC-Council training.
Cost: $1,699 and $2,049 depending on testing location

GIAC Security Essentials Certification (GSEC)

This certification from the Global Information Assurance Certification (GIAC) is an entry-level security credential for those with some background in information systems and networking. Earning this credential validates your skills in security tasks like active defense, network security, cryptography, incident response, and cloud security.

Consider taking the GSEC exam if you have some background in IT and wish to move into cybersecurity. Job roles that use the skills demonstrated by the GSEC include:
- IT security manager - $119,246
- Computer forensic analyst - $86,856
- Penetration tester - $93,973
- Security administrator - $62,869
- IT auditor -$78,933
- Software development engineer - $114,559

Requirements: There are no specific requirements to take the GSEC exam. Set yourself up for success by gaining some information systems or computer networking experience first.
Cost: $1,299

Systems Security Certified Practitioner (SSCP)

With this intermediate security credential from (ISC)², you can show employers that you have the skills to design, implement, and monitor a secure IT infrastructure. The exam tests expertise in access controls, risk identification and analysis, security administration, incident response, cryptography, and network, communications, systems, and application security.

The SSCP is designed for IT professionals working hands-on with an organization's security systems or assets. This credential is appropriate for positions like:
- Network security engineer - $111,542
- System administrator - $78,885
- Systems engineer - $111,721
- Security analyst - $82,733
- Database administrator - $93,556
- Security consultant - $106,486

Requirements: Candidates for the SSCP need at least one year of paid work experience in one or more of the testing areas. This can also be satisfied with a bachelor's or master's degree in a cybersecurity-related program.
Cost: $249

CompTIA Advanced Security Practitioner (CASP+)

The CASP+ is designed for cybersecurity professionals who demonstrate advanced skills but want to continue working in technology (as opposed to management). The exam covers advanced topics like enterprise security domain, risk analysis, software vulnerability, securing cloud and virtualization technologies, and cryptographic techniques.

The CASP+ can open up opportunities for advanced roles in architecture, risk management, and enterprise security integration. Possible job titles include:
- Security architect - $149,722
- Security engineer - $106,141
- Application security engineer - $121,457
- Technical lead analyst - $121,584
- Vulnerability analyst - $96,313

Requirements: There's not a formal prerequisite for taking the CASP+ exam. CompTIA recommends it only for experienced cybersecurity professionals with at least ten years of IT administration experience (including five years of broad hands-on experience with security).
Cost: $494

GIAC Certified Incident Handler (GCIH)

Earning the GCIH validates your understanding of offensive operations, including common attack techniques and vectors and your ability to detect, respond, and defend against attacks. The certification exam covers incident handling, computer crime investigation, hacker exploits, and hacker tools.

This certification is meant for anyone working in incident response. Job titles include:
- Security incident handler - $67,441
- Security architect - $149,722
- System administrator - $78,885

Requirements: There are no formal prerequisites for taking the GCIH exam, though it's a good idea to have an understanding of security principles, networking protocols, and the Windows Command Line.
Cost: $949

Offensive Security Certified Professional (OSCP)

The OSCP from Offensive Security has become one of the most sought-after certifications for penetration testers. The exam tests your ability to compromise a series of target machines using multiple exploitation steps and produce detailed penetration test reports for each attack.

The OSCP is a good option for jobs like:
- Penetration tester - $93,973
- Ethical hacker -$105,548
- Threat researcher - $57,612
- Application security analyst - $96,140

Requirements: There are no formal requirements to take the exam. Offensive Security recommends familiarity with networking, Linux, Bash scripting, Perl or Python, as well as completion of the Penetration Testing with Kali course.
Cost: From $999 (Basic package includes Penetration Testing with Kali Linux course, 30 days of lab access, and one exam attempt).

Cybersecurity credentials and certifications are excellent to have as they validate your skills and provide a standardized benchmark that employers can use to assess candidates. So, while not strictly required, they are highly beneficial and often essential for a successful and competitive career.

The above professional certifications should be your go-to reference to build your career, both short term and long term. To get from the classroom to the boardroom, it is important to continue to enhance and develop new cybersecurity skills and proficiencies that will help you "climb the ladder".

4. HIRING TREND: DEGREES VS SKILLS

Which is better, a degree or skills from a cybersecurity certificate?

With each passing year, cyber-attacks are getting more sophisticated and common. The costs of these attacks are also increasing, with the average data breach now totaling $9.44 million, according to a recent study by IBM.

Demand for cybersecurity professionals is at an all-time high and is only going to increase. It certainly is a good time for those that have cybersecurity skills and degrees to enter the job market.

To start a cybersecurity career or transition into the field, it is recommended to do a quick self-assessment. Cybersecurity concepts can be learned, but it will help if you already possess some of the skill. Anyone with an excellent approach to problem-solving and attention to detail already has entry-level cybersecurity skills. With the right kind of thinking and a solid work ethic, you could already be well on your way to a fast-paced, rewarding career.

Considering any career, whether you're just entering the workforce or looking for a new job, can raise some concerns. You may wonder if it's the right move or if you should choose something else. However, there's never been a better time to start your career in cybersecurity. It's a career with and opportunities in several different roles. For example, information security analyst jobs are predicted to grow by 32% between now and 2032 (U.S. Bureau of Labor Statistics).

What are the essential skills needed for cyber security? At the top of the list are problem-solving skills. Day in and day out, cybersecurity professionals are called to address complex issues in creative ways. New information security threats always emerge, requiring cybersecurity pros to think quickly and apply their existing knowledge. Attention to detail, strong analytical skills, and the ability to evaluate the most minute details go a long way in a cybersecurity career.

As a cybersecurity worker, you'll need excellent communication skills. You'll work with many different people in a wide range of roles from nearly every department. The ability to clearly explain security issues, their impact, and how to address them is critical. At specific points, you'll be required to speak in technical language. At others, you'll need to explain things in ways that your non-technical co-workers can understand.

Your next move should be to look for a certification(s), like presented in the previous chapter, that not only equips you with the foundational technical aspects of cybersecurity but also provides thorough hands-on practice. The best courses will provide lab time so that you can learn and practice in real-world scenarios while building problem-solving skills.

Capture the Flag (CTF) exercises help build technical skills required for cybersecurity. In addition to labs, CTFs are a great way to hone your analytical thinking skills while gaining technical experience. EC-Council's Certified Cybersecurity Technician (C|CT) course features all the components needed to learn essential cybersecurity skills.

Cybersecurity Degrees

A cybersecurity degree is a four-year program typically offered by colleges and universities. These programs can provide students with a more in-depth understanding of cybersecurity concepts and systems. In addition to taking classes on cybersecurity topics, students in cybersecurity degree programs also complete coursework in areas like computer science, mathematics, and engineering. This broad range of coursework gives students the opportunity to develop a well-rounded skill set that can be applied to many cybersecurity positions. These degree programs can also benefit people who want to move into management and leadership positions or are interested in research and development roles.

In addition, advanced degrees offer opportunities for current and future cybersecurity professionals to gain both theoretical knowledge and hands-on experience, cybersecurity master's degree programs are increasingly regarded as a providing a powerful competitive edge in the employment market. Capstone-type programs that simulate real-world cybersecurity projects are designed not only to give students valuable experience, but also the ability to demonstrate a meaningful work product to potential employers during a job search.

Skills from Cybersecurity Certificates

A cybersecurity certificate is a short-term program that can be completed in as little as six months. These programs are typically offered by technical schools, community colleges, and online providers. Most cybersecurity certificate programs cover the basics of cybersecurity and provide students with the opportunity to gain hands-on experience with various cybersecurity tools and systems. Many certificate programs also offer specializations in areas like network security or digital forensics. Certificate programs are a good option for people who are already working in the IT field and want to transition into cybersecurity or for those looking to jump-start their cybersecurity careers.

As explained in the previous chapter, industry certifications have become an essential component of the cybersecurity ecosystem. They help current and aspiring cybersecurity professionals gain knowledge and sought-after skills in key areas, they enhance your profile when reaching out to prospective employers and are often listed as required or preferred for jobs.

Cybersecurity Degree vs Skills from Cybersecurity Certificates

The main difference between a cybersecurity degree and a certificate in cybersecurity is the time commitment, the knowledge gained, and the cost. That said, even if you decide to pursue a cybersecurity degree, you should continue learning after earning it. Gaining a degree should eventually prompt you to pursue certifications, as they can keep your knowledge and skills fresh in your chosen cybersecurity field.

Time: A conventional cybersecurity degree program is four years long. That is eight semesters of full-time study at a rate of five classes per semester. Taking five classes per semester will need at least 15 hours per week of class time, not counting time spent on homework, studying, and in labs. A master's degree in cybersecurity could add another year or more to this schedule. Taking a full course load on top of 40 or more hours of work per week may not be practical if you are employed full-time. If you opt to pursue a cybersecurity degree while working full-time, you may decide to take only one or two courses per semester, prolonging the time required to earn that degree. On the other hand, certifications provide more specific training in less time. Certification can take up to six months to obtain, depending on the chosen cybersecurity field. This makes it much easier for full-time employees to gain knowledge in a given area.

Affordability: EducationData reports the average cost of one year of in-state tuition at a public four-year college is just over $9,300. The average cost of one year at a private, four-year college or university is over $37,000. This is just for tuition. These figures will increase significantly with the addition of textbooks, laboratories, dormitory rooms, and meal plans. However, certifications cost a fraction of that. Most certification fees cover the cost of the certification exam as well as the cost of any required study materials. This might cost anything from $100 to $2,000, depending on the type of certification.

So, which is better: a cybersecurity degree or skills acquired from cybersecurity certificates? The answer to this question depends on your career goals, previous job experience, free time, and price. A degree program may be a better fit if you are interested in pursuing a career in cybersecurity and want a comprehensive education in the field. A degree program may be a better fit if you are interested in pursuing a career in cybersecurity and want a comprehensive education in the field. However, pursuing this degree can be time-consuming, and for those working full-time, it can last even longer than four years. Ultimately, the best option for you will depend on your specific goals and needs.

Alternatively, certificate program may be a good option if you are already working in the IT field and want to transition into cybersecurity. It is also great for those with little to no experience in cybersecurity who want to start.

While having a degree in cybersecurity can be helpful and increase your chances of being hired in the field, it is not always necessary. Some employers may prioritize skills and experience over formal education. However, having a degree can provide a solid foundation in the field, teach you important concepts, and provide opportunities for internships and networking. It is important to note that the cybersecurity field is constantly evolving, and keeping up with the latest trends and technologies is crucial to staying competitive, regardless of whether you have a degree or not.

Working in cybersecurity does not necessarily require a degree. It requires skills you can prove. The challenge you will face is twofold. The degree and certifications only get you past the Human Resource screeners. So, getting the interviews might be a little tricky. Second, is that there are not many entry level positions in cybersecurity. The only real way onto a cybersecurity team is to have experience and credentials or to work your way onto one laterally.

A person with no experience would have to start at the helpdesk and do six months to a year there. And then try and get promoted off helpdesk and onto an admin team. Do another six months to a year on the admin team and then try to get another promotion on to the engineering team or possibly the cybersecurity team.

A lot of this depends on how you work with the other teams and what you do while you are a member of the helpdesk or admin teams.

You should make friends with members or management on the cybersecurity team. Perhaps volunteer for some projects working with them. Cultivate skills they are looking for as you grow your profile in the organization and then try to slide laterally into a cybersecurity position.

5. INTERNSHIPS AND APPRENTICESHIPS

Internships and apprenticeships could be a great way to enter the cybersecurity job market.

An internship is a form of experiential learning that integrates knowledge and theory learned in the classroom with practical application and skills development in a professional/organization setting.

An apprenticeship is a work-based learning model where apprentices have supervised on-the-job training, along with job-related education, all while earning a wage that increases during the progression of the program. Apprenticeship programs are intended for long-term employment.

U.S. Homeland Security has some good internship and apprenticeship programs to look into.

The U.S. Homeland Security Cybersecurity Internship Program is designed to give current high school and college students an opportunity to work alongside cyber leaders with the U.S. Department of Homeland Security. Interns are recruited from the nation's high school, undergraduate, and graduate programs and have the opportunity to apply concepts, protocols and tools acquired through coursework in the real world by working with cybersecurity/information technology experts or in cybersecurity/information technology support areas. Internships focus on U.S. Homeland Security mission areas and include identification and analysis of malicious code, forensics analysis, incident handling, intrusion detection and prevention, software assurance, data management, cloud/web services, and network operations.

Also, search cybersecurity internship and you'll see listings on Linkedin, Indeed and elsewhere, and you'll find interesting opportunities in a wide variety of positions.

The U.S. Homeland Security Cybersecurity Apprenticeship Program (CSAP) is designed to give current students an opportunity to work alongside cyber leaders at the U.S. Department of Homeland Security (DHS). Hosted by the DHS Headquarters Office of the Chief Information Officer, CSAP offers apprentices part-time positions throughout the agency. By working side by side with experts in cybersecurity, apprentices can gain valuable work experience and apply concepts, protocols and tools acquired through their academic achievements.

Internship or Apprenticeship: Which One Is Right for You?

Internships are typically ideal for people who are early in their professional journey and who may want to gain general workplace experience. Often, internships don't focus on developing a specific skill set so it can be ideal for someone who may want to see what it's like to work in a particular field of industry before applying to organizations.

Apprenticeships are great for those who have an interest in a certain field or industry and want to gain hands-on skills with the intent of working in that area for the long term. Apprenticeships can be good for those who are considering switching fields or who may not want to pursue a traditional collegiate route.

Finding an internship or apprenticeship could be exactly the right step toward a successful career in cybersecurity. Use these resources to find one that interests you.

Resources for Finding Internships

Internships are often listed similar to job opportunities. Here are some different resources to consider when searching for an internship:

- Schools: Schools and colleges frequently partner with local companies to help students find opportunities. Check with your school's career services or talk to a faculty member to see what internships they have available.
- Job fairs: Local job fairs can be a good resource. It also gives you an opportunity to see what's available and get a feel for different companies and industries.
- Internship websites: There are certain websites focused solely on internships, including sites such as Internships.com.
- Research career websites: Sites such as Indeed, ZipRecruiter, Handshake, and Glassdoor often post internship opportunities along with job openings.
- Social media: Linkedin is a good resource for finding internships. You can also post your need for an internship on other social media sites. It's possible that your network may be able to help you find an opportunity.

Resources for Finding Apprenticeships

Apprenticeships are government-regulated programs so there are lots of resources for finding an opportunity, including:

- CompTIA Apprenticeships for Tech: CompTIA helps connect workers with opportunities in the tech industry.
- Apprenticeship USA: A government website, Apprenticeship USA is a great resource for finding accredited programs in technology.
- Indeed Paid Apprenticeship: Indeed has an apprenticeship filter that allows you to just search for paid apprenticeships.
- Career One Stop: Sponsored by the U.S. Department of Labor. Career One Stop helps you find apprenticeship opportunities.
- NICE Cybersecurity Apprenticeship Program Finder: NICE helps you find cybersecurity-specific programs near you.

With both the internship and apprenticeship route, you will learn skills that are directly relevant to a career in cybersecurity, and gain work experience, which can help you land the job.

6. DIGITAL ACHIEVEMENT WALLET

A digital achievement wallet is an interoperable application technology that provides the users (wallet-holders) with the ability to curate, customize, and share credentials, skill, education, work history and achievements with prospective employers, career services, and on social media. It provides the wallet-holder with the ability to showcase their unique talent brand, based on the credentials they hold and the skills they have demonstrated. Because of the power of the skills architecture, the achievement wallet also has compassing capabilities to reveal both career and educational pathway insights based on current skillset, career goals, and educational aspirations.

iQ4 Corporation, a technology company, has developed a digital achievement wallet software product, that includes a live job search capability, for full-time jobs, internships, and apprenticeships. All based on the wallet-holders geo-location preference. The wallet-holder can apply to the jobs they are matched to, real-time.

iQ4 uses in its software product "Athena", powerful algorithms and programs that combine artificial intelligence and machine learning, resulting in the capability to match a wallet-holder's skills to job requisition postings by employers. Employers use an iQ4 application called the Enterprise Skills Talent Pipeline to load their job requisition into it, and Athena does the matching and identifies the wallet-holders that meet the skills in the job requisitions. Employers can then contact the top candidates to discuss job opportunities.

Athena offers tools for analyzing current skills, exploring potential career paths, identifying necessary skills for desired roles, finding educational resources, and receiving personalized learning recommendations.

Questions a user of the iQ4 Achievement Wallet will have answered are:

- Where am I at with my skills and proficiencies?
- How can I evaluate my current skills and understand where I stand in terms of my professional development?
- Where can I go (future job role exploration)?
- What are all the different career paths I can explore, and what are the opportunities available to me for the future?

- What do I need for my career journey?
- How do I figure out what skills I am missing that are necessary for the roles I aspire to take on?
- Where can I acquire the courses/training that I need?
- What are all the courses, training programs, or resources to learn the skills I need?
- How can I get tailored advice or recommendations on what to learn next, based on my career goals and current skill set?

Following are Screen-Shots of the iQ4 Digital Achievement Wallet.

[Registration, Resume/Military Transcript Uploaded
(Skills, Credentials, Education, Work History)](#)

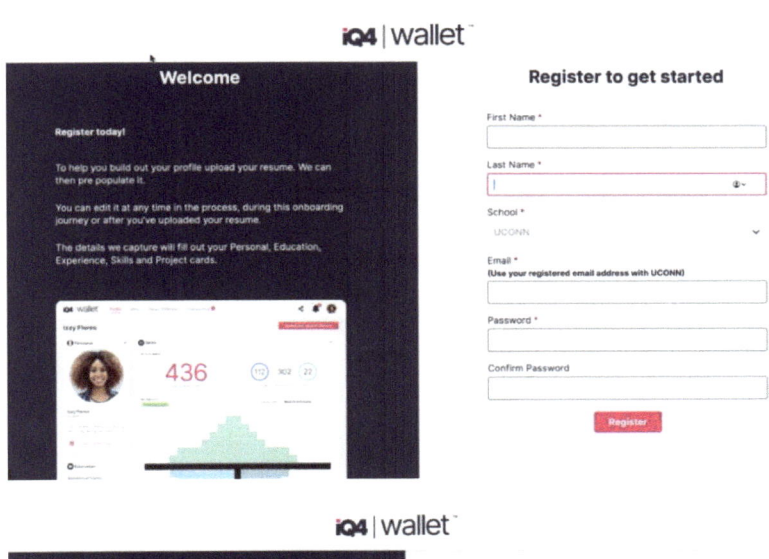

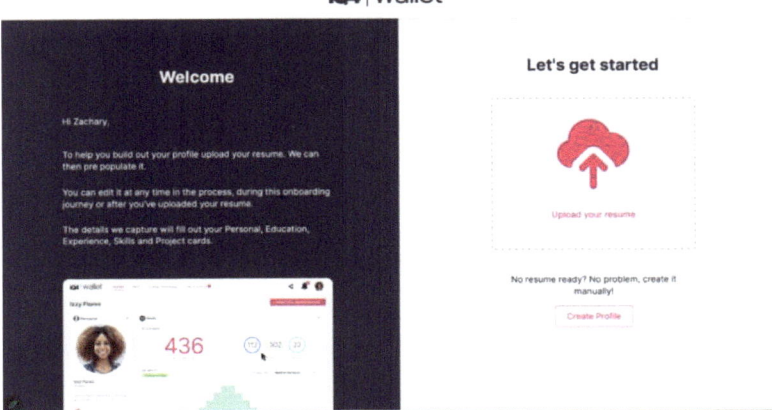

Digital Achievement Wallet Main Page

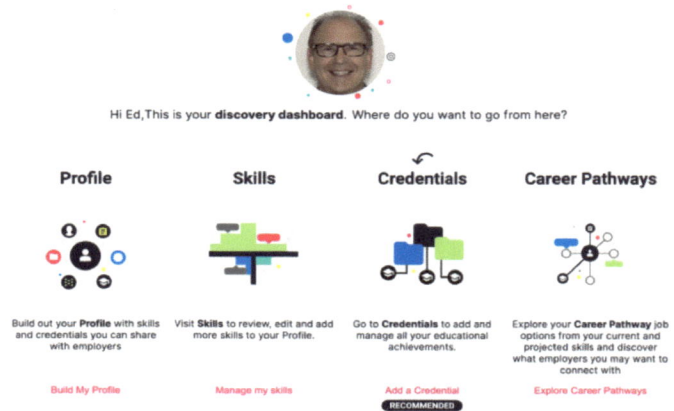

Education, Work Experience, Skills displayed and T-Shape

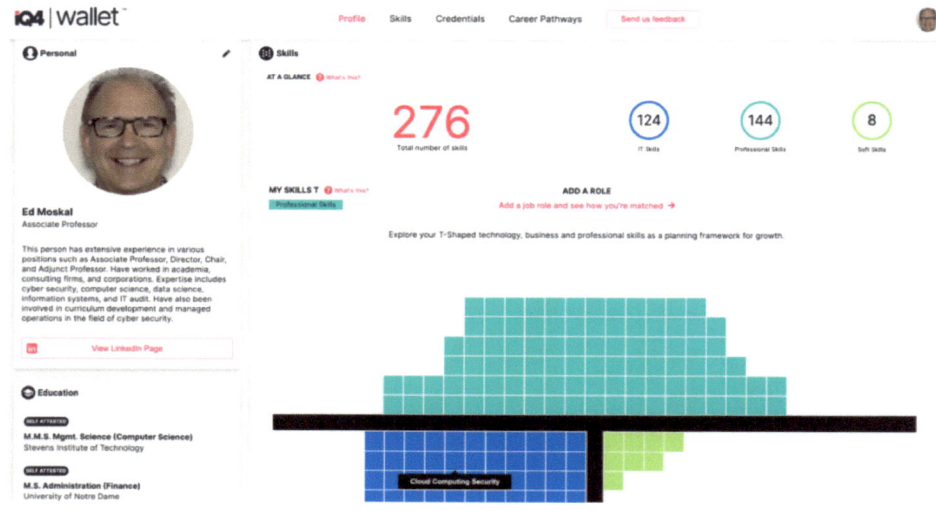

Search for any Job to see where the Job Skills Align with yours

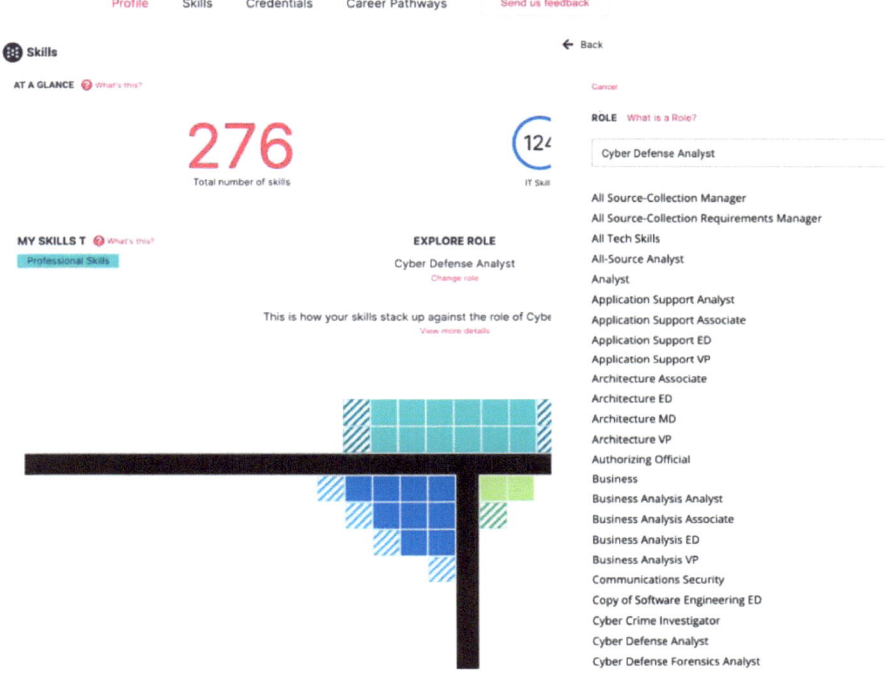

Change Job Family

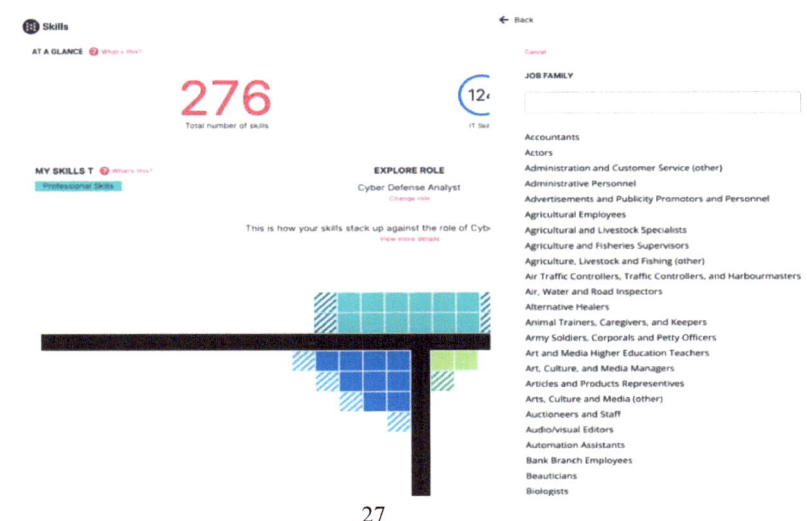

CAREER PATHWAYS IN CYBER SECURITY: FROM CLASSROOM TO BOARDROOM

Hover over a Skill and you will see if you have it or not.
(Solid Box = have Skill. Stripe Box = do not have Skill.)

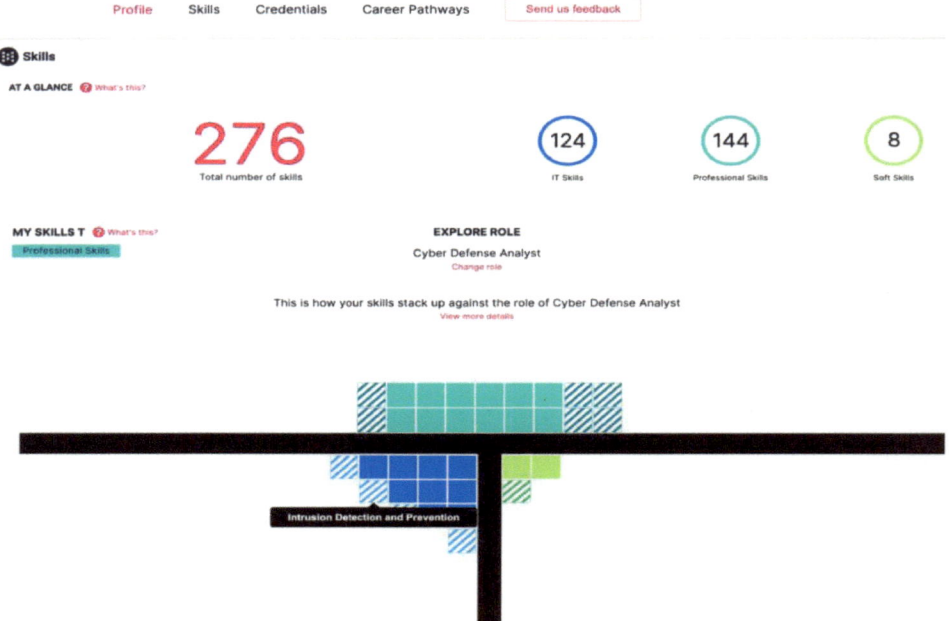

See all your Skills, Select Skill Details, Conduct a Self-Assessment

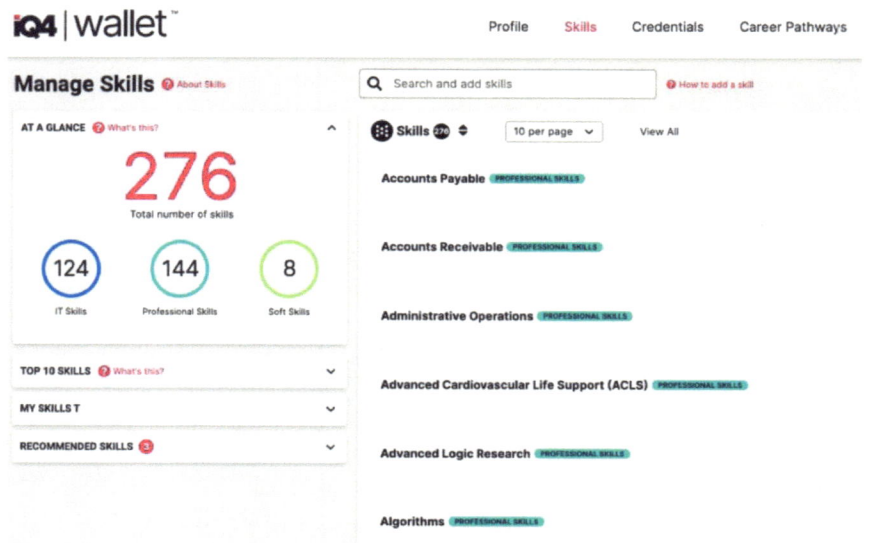

Algorithms

PROFESSIONAL SKILLS

🗑 Delete this skill   ⊘ Hide this Skill from recommending roles

Algorithms is a specialized skill that involves developing a logical process or a set of rules to solve a problem or perform a particular task. It entails ide efficiently and optimizing them to minimize time complexity and maximize performance. Algorithms are used in various fields such as computer scienc expertise in data structures, programming languages, and problem-solving techniques. Developing effective algorithms is a critical skill for software de professionals who work with large datasets and complex systems.

⁝⁞ SKILL DETAILS   ★ PROFICIENCY   ♀ SOURCES   ⌾ LEARNING RESOURCES

☐ Explain complex mathematical models and algorithms.
☐ Write different algorithms for sorting a list.
☐ Write recursive functions.
☐ Explain the logic and structure of simple algorithms.
☐ Explain the differences between distinct types of algorithms.
☐ Apply models and algorithms to solve new and unique business problems.
☐ Write algorithms that create economic solutions for a company through calculation performance, data processing, and automated reasoning.
☐ Algorithms

Algorithms

PROFESSIONAL SKILLS

🗑 Delete this skill   ⊘ Hide this Skill from recommending roles

Algorithms is a specialized skill that involves developing a logical process or a set of rules to solve efficiently and optimizing them to minimize time complexity and maximize performance. Algorithms expertise in data structures, programming languages, and problem-solving techniques. Developing professionals who work with large datasets and complex systems.

⁝⁞ SKILL DETAILS   ★ PROFICIENCY   ♀ SOURCES   ⌾ LEARNING RESOURCES

YOUR SELF ASSESSMENT ⓘ

👤 ★★★★

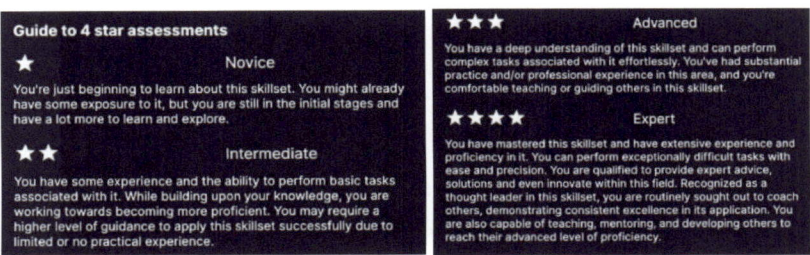

Add Credentials from 3rd Party Providers/Professional Certifications

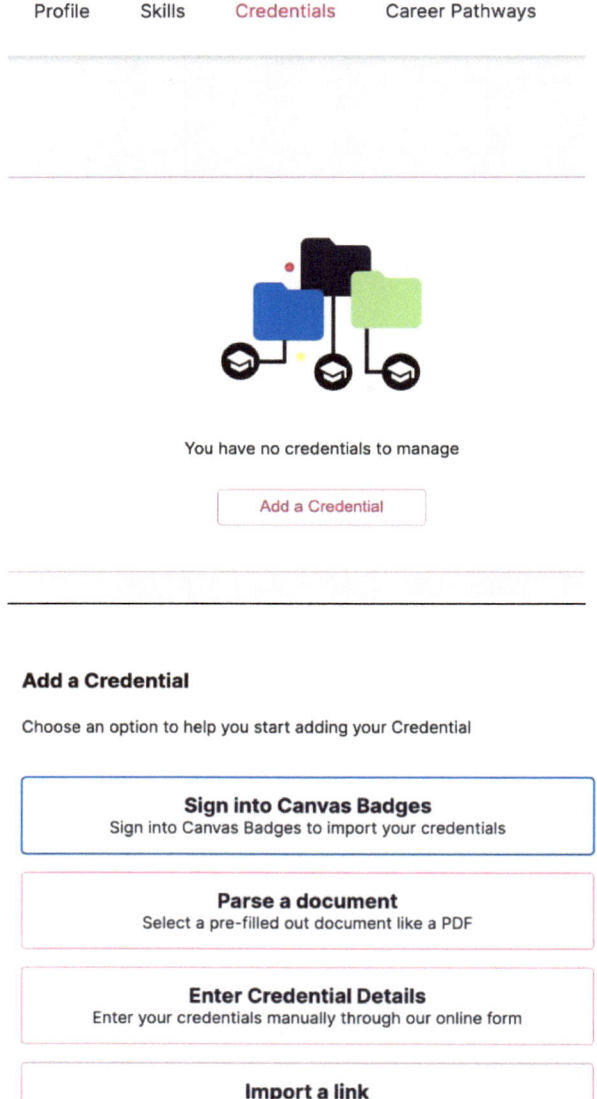

Search for Jobs by Geographic Area

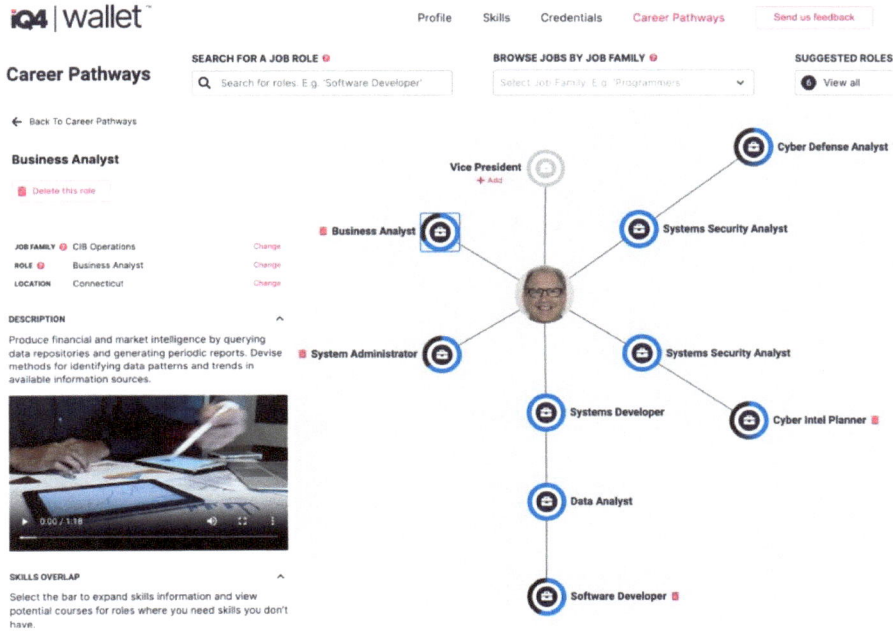

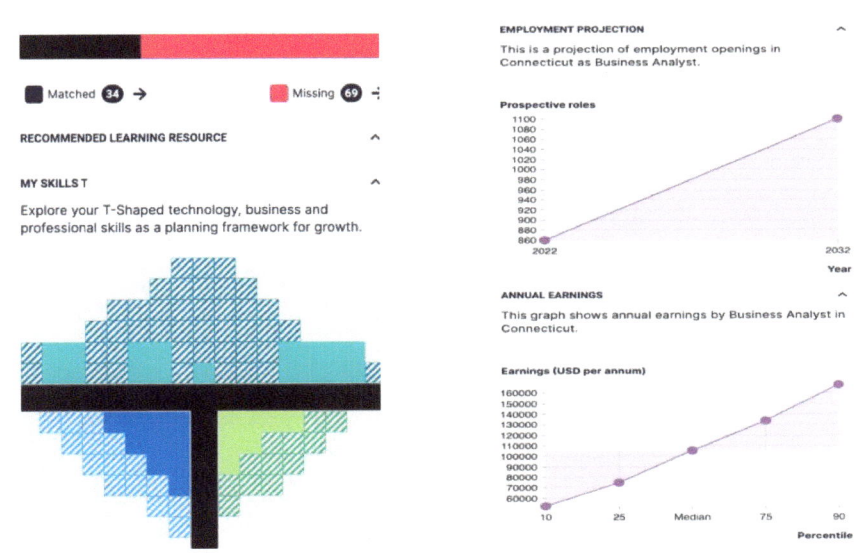

CAREER PATHWAYS IN CYBER SECURITY: FROM CLASSROOM TO BOARDROOM

Job Search - Full Time or Internships

LIVE ROLES

☐ Show Internships only

Data & Reporting Professional, SPARx
Humana
📍 Hartford, CT — Learn More

Developer, Business Intelligence
WM
📍 Hartford, CT — Learn More

Senior Marketing Data Analyst
PagerDuty
📍 Hartford, CT — Learn More

Sr Mgr Business Intelligence & Rptg- Business Resilence Reporting
TD Bank

LIVE ROLES

☑ Show Internships only

Signify Geomode Analyst Corporate Intern - Summer 2024
CVS Health
📍 Hartford, CT — Learn More

Senior Analyst, Internal Audit
CVS Health
📍 Hartford, CT — Learn More

Signify Geomode Analyst Corporate Intern - Summer 2024
CVS Health
📍 Hartford, CT — Learn More

JD Intern - Public International Law
Pacific Northwest National Laboratory

Select Job you are Interested in and Apply to it

What

job title, keywords

Home   **View All Jobs** (726)

Where

Bloomfield, CT

city, state, country

Business Analytics Senior Advisor – Medicare Growth Analytics - Cigna Healthcare - Remote in Bloomfield, Connecticut

Remote - Work from home - United States

Summary

The Business Analytics Senior Advisor position within the Medicare Growth Analytics Team is an opportunity to provide leadership on our analytics strategy, to support our broader Medicare Growth team and provide actionable insights and analytics. This role will work with a team of professionals on setting and executing the vision for how our Medicare Growth team can lead Cigna to achieving its goals.

Reporting to the Cross Channel Analytics Senior Manager, this position will coordinate with cross functional teams to develop and execute key deliverables with our business stakeholders. This position will blend creativity, analytical, and technical competencies, relentless problem solving, and business acumen to deliver solutions to our business partners. The focus of the work will be on analytical projects including but not limited to: Medicare Growth, Medicare Conversions, Customer Lifetime Value, Customer Retention, and Competitive Analysis.

We are seeking a seasoned professional for the role of Business Analytics Senior Advisor to spearhead our data integration, modeling, and analytics efforts. Collaborating closely with the Medicare Growth team, you will play a pivotal role in shaping our data strategy and delivering advanced solutions for key growth reports and strategic analyses. This is a growth position requiring expertise, vision, and a track record of success in driving data-driven initiatives.

Responsibilities

- Provides expert content/professional leadership on complex analytics assignments/projects.
- Exercises considerable creativity, foresight, and judgement in conceiving and delivering initiatives.
- Takes projects from beginning to end by managing variable tasks, stakeholder engagement and data review with limited supervision to meet targeted timelines.
- Analyzes results and presents data in a consumable method using high-level overviews, major takeaways, critical questions, and next steps. Partners with other analytics and growth team members to make executive-level recommendations and align on strategy and plan.
- Enhances understanding of distribution channel performance and its impact on

iQ4 has created an eco-system/a talent cloud that provides the ability to translate someone's background: resumes, military transcripts, credentials into skills, career pathways and jobs. Athena's matching and pathways engine are core. The iQ4 Digital Achievement Wallet creates a supply chain for human capital, enabling a Learning and Employment Record infrastructure, resulting in a skill's marketplace.

Here is a QR code and URL to a demo of the iQ4 Digital Achievement Wallet:

https://www.youtube.com/watch?v=cVp4F3O9JYE

For more information or to get your iQ4 Digital Achievement Wallet email:

info@iq4.com

www.iQ4.com

7. HOW TO LAND THE JOB

Most cybersecurity job requirements pertain to your knowledge of the role. College, immersive bootcamps, certifications, and self-education can equip you with the skills you need in network security, systems administration and security auditing and response.

Internships and apprenticeships allow you to learn from seasoned cybersecurity professionals and gain hands-on experience. They can give you a competitive edge over applicants who have no experience at all.

A cybersecurity portfolio cements your credibility as an information security professional with skills and experience. To build your portfolio, consider working on open-source cybersecurity projects, participating in hackathons and sharing your knowledge on public platforms. You can host your projects in a private GitHub repository and grant access to hiring managers on demand.

Gaining professional work experience is the best way to jumpstart a cybersecurity career. You can find entry-level cybersecurity positions on job boards, company websites and social media platforms like Linkedin.

U.S. citizens can also apply for cybersecurity jobs with the federal government via USAJobs.

Earn cybersecurity certifications. These credentials can improve your marketability as a candidate. As you gain more full-time work experience, plan to earn relevant industry certifications as well.

Experts describe the cybersecurity job landscape as "a seller's market" with zero percent unemployment, as organizations across all industries offer high salaries for top talent. Salaries for entry-level cybersecurity jobs also run significantly higher than in many other industries attracting new talent to this vitally important and fast-moving field.

However, research shows that even many entry-level cybersecurity jobs require 3-5 years of related experience. According to a "State of Cybersecurity Hiring Report" from Burning Glass Technologies, "Most cybersecurity employers aren't looking for newbies, and they aren't looking for those without a college degree, either. Some 88% of cybersecurity postings specify at least a bachelor's degree or higher, and roughly the same percent demand at least three years of experience."

So how do you get your foot in the cybersecurity job market door?

One thing that is definitely working in your favor: Businesses and government agencies of all shapes, sizes and missions are in need of cybersecurity professionals, and there just isn't enough talent to go around.

SecurityMagazine.com puts the situation in like this: The Cybersecurity Talent Gap = an Industry Crisis. This is definitely a time of opportunity.

Seven Key Cyber Workforce Categories to Focus on for Landing the Job

There is a broad range of different categories of cybersecurity jobs and the list of job duties and responsibilities is particular to the position and the organization in question.

One helpful resource comes from the U.S. government, among the world's largest cybersecurity employers. As part of its National Initiative for Cybersecurity Education (NICE), the National Institute of Standards and Technology (NIST) created a detailed set of guidelines to help private-sector organizations assess and improve their ability to prevent, detect and respond to cyberattacks.

This list from NICE breaks down cybersecurity roles into seven key workforce categories:

- Securely Provision (SP) - Conceptualizes, designs, procures, and/or builds secure information technology systems, with responsibility for aspects of system and/or network development.
- Operate and Maintain (OM) - Provides the support, administration, and maintenance necessary to ensure effective and efficient information technology system performance and security.
- Oversee and Govern (OV) - Provides leadership, management, direction, or development and advocacy so the organization may effectively conduct cybersecurity work.
- Protect and Defend (PR) - Identifies, analyzes, and mitigates threats to internal information technology systems and/or networks.
- Analyze (AN) - Performs highly specialized review and evaluation of incoming cybersecurity information to determine its usefulness for intelligence.

- Collect and Operate (CO) - Provides specialized denial and deception operations and collection of cybersecurity information that may be used to develop intelligence.
- Investigate (IN) - Investigates cybersecurity events or crimes related to information technology systems, networks, and digital evidence.

Cybersecurity Career Paths: Feeder Roles into Entry-Level Cyber Jobs

Your pathway into an entry-level cybersecurity job can include work experience in a variety of different domains. However, these are generally considered to be the top five feeder roles:

- Networking
- Software development
- Systems engineering
- Financial and risk analysis
- Security intelligence

One good resource to better understand such feeder roles and how they create opportunities to transition into entry-level and then upper-level cybersecurity jobs is provided by CyberSeek.org. Their Cybersecurity Career Pathway tool includes detailed information about the salaries, credentials and skillsets associated with various roles.

CyberSeek's Career Pathway tool lists four fundamental entry-level cybersecurity jobs. Here is a look at each of them:

Cybersecurity Specialist/Technician

- Key skills and knowledge requested: information security, information systems, information assurance, network security, security operations, vulnerability assessment, project management, Linux, NIST cybersecurity framework.
- Related job titles: information security specialist, IT security specialist, IT specialist – information security
- Top certifications requested: CompTIA Security+, Certified Information Systems Security Professional (CISSP), SANS/GIAC Certification, Certified Information Systems Auditor (CISA), Certified Information Security Manager (CISM)
- Average salary: $92,000

Cyber Crime Analyst/Investigator

- Key skills and knowledge requested: computer forensics, Linux, information security, consumer electronics, hard drives, information systems, forensic toolkit, UNIX, malware engineering
- Related job titles: digital forensics analyst, cyber forensic specialist, cybersecurity forensic analyst, computer forensics analyst
- Top certifications requested: SANS/GIAC Certification, CISSP, EnCase Certified Examiner (EnCE), GIAC Certified Forensic Analyst, GIAC Certified Incident Handler (GCIH)
- Average salary: $94,000

Incident Analyst/Responder

- Key skills and knowledge requested: information security, project management, information systems, Linux, network security, technical support, intrusion detection, UNIX, security operations
- Related job titles: information security analyst, disaster recovery specialist, network technical specialist, audit project manager
- Top certifications requested: CompTIA Security+, CISSP, SANS/GIAC Certification, GIAC Certified Incident Handler, IT Infrastructure Library (ITIL) Certification
- Average salary: $89,000

IT Auditor

- Key skills and knowledge requested: internal auditing, audit planning, information systems, Sarbanes-Oxley (SOX), accounting, risk assessment, information security, COBIT, business process
- Related job titles: IT audit consultant, IT audit manager, IT internal auditor, senior IT auditor
- Top certifications requested: Certified Information Systems Auditor (CISA), CISSP, CISM, ITIL, Information Systems Certification
- Average salary: $98,000

Other entry-level cybersecurity jobs include:

- Information security analyst
- Junior penetration tester
- Systems administrator
- Security technician

The bar for what constitutes an entry level position in cybersecurity tends to be significantly higher than in many other industries. According to the National Security Agency (NSA), entry level for many cybersecurity positions means:

- Bachelor's degree plus 3 years of relevant experience
- Master's degree plus 1 year of relevant experience
- Doctoral degree and no experience
- Associate degree plus 5 years of in-depth experience clearly related to the position.

The NSA is also a high-profile example of how the ongoing need for talent has inspired numerous organizations to recruit and groom people for entry-level cybersecurity that can position you for many career opportunities going forward.

On its Cyber Careers page, the NSA informs potential cyber recruits that "you will become a part of a tradition of excellence, poised to lead the nation in the protection of our country's national interests in cyberspace for years to come." Its recruiting efforts place particular emphasis on skills in computer science, intelligence analysis, mathematics, and engineering.

The agency offers well over a dozen paid, three-year career development programs in cybersecurity and other fields designed to help employees enhance their skills and cross-train for new careers. Such programs represent an excellent opportunity to gain the type of experience that so many cybersecurity-focused employers are looking for.

Now some tips on how to stand-out when applying for a cybersecurity job:

Speak the language: Develop a thorough understanding of all the key industry terms and acronyms. It's essential that you work toward becoming fluent in the technical language used by cybersecurity professionals.

Get qualified: Take the initiative to do some self-learning through certification.

Network: Whether through school, certification programs or old-fashioned legwork, look for and leverage opportunities to converse with people who are working in the field. Seek out cybersecurity groups and meetups, both in-person and virtual.

Document your training and skills: Put extra effort into making sure that your resume strongly showcases the work you have put in to prepare yourself for cybersecurity opportunities. Another great way to stand out is to have the sharpest-looking personal webpage so you can engage potential employers with not only your qualifications but your online creativity.

Be prepared: When applying for a specific job, do some homework to gather information on what the job is all about. Knowing what the job requires enables you to develop strategies for talking about your abilities to do the work.

Ask intelligent questions: In many interviews, the interviewer will invite you to ask him or her any questions. So don't be caught off guard; ask something that shows an understanding of and a curiosity about the role for which you're applying.

Stay informed: Read regularly publishes journals and articles to connect you with additional cybersecurity job tips and resources such as the top cybersecurity blogs and websites to keep an eye on.

8. WORKING WITH OTHERS

It is often said that cybersecurity is a team sport. Cybersecurity functions are usually made up of multiple teams. Those teams interact with other teams within an organization. Sometimes your teams might have to form ad-hoc teams to solve pressing problems, like responding to an incident.

Effective cybersecurity requires a coordinated and collaborative approach between different teams in IT and security. Working in teams allows for a more comprehensive approach to cybersecurity, with each team member bringing their unique expertise and skillset to the table.

The biggest reason why cybersecurity must be a collaborative effort is because siloes breed vulnerabilities. You can't secure what you can't see, yet 60% of security software users analyze less than 40% of their log data.

A cybersecurity workplace culture is a culture where security is ingrained and infused in every aspect of the workplace. It is built into thinking and planning. It is included in the application, systems, and processes. It is a part and parcel of how work is done. Thereby, minimizing the chances of a cyber-attack.
A strong cybersecurity posture is heavily reliant on an organization's culture. Building a cybersecurity workplace culture not only emphasizes and reinforces security behaviors among staff but also helps to protect your organization against a cyber-attack.

Establishing a cybersecurity workplace culture, while widely considered to be a tough mission to accomplish, is not as daunting as you may think.

Consider a few elements, the first of which is attitude. The attitude towards cybersecurity, including how the management implements cybersecurity while ensuring educational and communication plans are in place; all contribute to successfully building a cybersecurity workplace culture.

<u>Check C-Level Attitudes Toward Cyber Security</u>

An organization's attitude towards cybersecurity, as a collective, plays a significant role in how employees incorporate it into their everyday work behavior. It is neither fair nor realistic to expect the frontline to be motivated about cybersecurity if the C-Suite, senior leadership, and management are not committed to the mission.

Therefore, it is mandatory that organizational leadership and management at all levels build a positive attitude around cybersecurity awareness and encourage the workforce to become enthusiastic about building a culture of cybersecurity. Achieving this enhances the employee's awareness, consequently, the ability to minimize cyber risks. Every workplace is faced with cyber risks and cyber threats. The right attitude helps drive appropriate behaviors across the entire organization and at all levels.

Management Must Lead

Organizational leadership and senior management set the tone in organizations. They influence the mindsets of others. They can help generate awareness for the factors and issues that matter. If leadership and management embrace cybersecurity as a priority and propagate it as a message, it will be taken more seriously. Leadership and management training on relevant components of cybersecurity and training for middle management and frontline on cybersecurity enhances awareness and mitigates risk. Transfer of cybersecurity knowledge and best practices within the workplace also help enhance awareness and reduce cyber risks.

Leadership and management must support investments related to cybersecurity initiatives, and they must model good personal security habits based on guidelines distributed throughout the workplace. Leaders play a key role in building a cybersecurity workplace culture. They also play a key role in helping drive the implementation of cybersecurity practices in the workplace.

Education is Key

Once management implements a cyber-security-conscious culture, the next step is to achieve employee awareness and training through various programs. Information technology is very much doing its job protecting organizations, and it is everyone else letting the team down, so employee awareness and training are essential. The training will assist in building an understanding of the risks and how to avoid cyber-attacks. Too often employees are caught off guard and unaware giving cybercriminals an unfair advantage.

Plan Ahead – Stay Ahead of Attackers

Senior staff and managers must develop a communications plan for an inevitable cyberattack incident. If employees receive regular information on the cyber incident response plan, this will assist them in incorporating it into their overall workplace culture. A communication plan consistent with regulatory requirements, legal considerations, industry best practices, and commitments made to external stakeholders must be made available to all employees.

This plan must be created with the least tech-savvy staff in mind. It must include simple, vital information such as how to protect shared folders with encryptions and passwords. Such a plan must take into account commonly used applications that contain large amounts of sensitive data, such as Customer Relationship Management platforms. All staff should be required to use best-in-class practices for accessing cloud platforms, such as creating strong passphrases, using multi-factor authentication, and restricting access to those who need it. The more information your staff has on how to keep data safe, the better your chances of surviving an attack without a severe data leak.

No plan will ensure a 100% success rate against human-based activities, but substantially reducing the risk can help manage incidents. Internal awareness campaigns can also be used to help build a cyber-secure culture. Material such as posters, newsletters, and reminders are effective ways to generate "buzz" around important security themes.

Cybersecurity is Everyone's Responsibility

To be successful in creating an enriched cybersecurity environment continuous effort and emphasis on cybersecurity in the workplace must be practiced. Cybersecurity in the workplace is everyone's responsibility. Regardless of which approach is used to implement cybersecurity practices, you have to keep your employees interested, engaged, and invested in the process by making it fun, relatable, relevant, and simple.

Every individual in the workplace should ensure they exercise caution when using information systems and seek guidance from responsible individuals. They must understand how their work addresses cybersecurity risks, attend training and learn about the ever-evolving cyber-attack landscape, and know how to handle, store, transfer and dispose of information in the workplace.

Safeguarding assets like computers, mobile devices, and non-electronic information must be a priority, and adhering to workplace security procedures is essential. Together everyone in the workplace can make a difference to enhance cybersecurity.

Summary

Working with others (cybersecurity collaboration), is powerful in combating the ever-growing challenges of cyber threats. By working together, organizations can leverage shared knowledge, resources, and expertise to enhance threat detection, improve incident response, and strengthen their overall security posture.

9. REFERENCES

Burning Glass
State of Cybersecurity Hiring Report
https://paper.bobylive.com/Security/Annual_Report/2019/recruiting_watchers_cybersecurity_hiring.pdf

Career One Stop
Apprenticeship Programs
https://www.careeronestop.org/FindTraining/Types/apprenticeships.aspx

CompTIA
Information Technology Training and Certifications
https://www.comptia.org/

Credential Engine
Learning and Employment Record (LER) Guide
https://credreg.net/quickstart/lerguide

Cybersecurity Ventures
Cybersecurity Workforce Shortfall
https://cybersecurityventures.com/jobs/

Cyber Seek
U.S. Job Heat Map
https://www.cyberseek.org/heatmap.html

Cyber Seek
U.S. Job Career Pathways
https://www.cyberseek.org/pathway.html

EC-Council
Top Skills Required to Start Your Career in Cybersecurity
https://www.eccouncil.org/cybersecurity-exchange/cybersecurity-technician/

Education Data Initiative
Average Cost of College
https://educationdata.org/average-cost-of-college

Fortinet
Cybersecurity Training Institute
https://www.fortinet.com/nse-training

GitHub
Cybersecurity Repository
https://github.com/topics/cybersecurity

Hiring Our Heroes - U.S. Chamber of Commerce Foundation
Helping Military and Veterans Transition to Civilian Life
https://www.hiringourheroes.org/

IBM
Cost of Data Breaches in 2023
https://www.ibm.com/reports/data-breach

Indeed
Cybersecurity Job Search Engine
https://www.indeed.com/

INVETS
Helping Veterans Transition to Civilian Life in Indiana
https://www.invets.org/

iQ4 Corporation
Product Offerings
https://www.iq4.com/products

ISACA
Information Systems Audit and Control Association
https://www.isaca.org/credentialing/

ISC2
Revealing New Opportunities in the Cybersecurity Workforce
https://www.isc2.org/research

Linkedin
Cybersecurity Job Search Engine
https://www.linkedin.com/

National Centers of Academic Excellence in Cybersecurity
Program Managed by NSA's National Cryptologic School
https://www.nsa.gov/Academics/Centers-of-Academic-Excellence/

NICE
National Initiative for Cybersecurity Education
https://www.cisa.gov/national-initiative-cybersecurity-education-nice-cybersecurity-workforce-framework

NICE Framework
Cybersecurity Workforce Framework Categories
https://niccs.cisa.gov/workforce-development/nice-framework

NIST
National Institute for Standards and Technology
https://www.nist.gov/

RSM
Cybersecurity Survey
https://rsmus.com/newsroom/2023/rsm-us-cybersecurity-special-report-highlights-volatile-threat-environment-as-more-middle-market-firms-report-having-cyber-insurance.html

SANS Institute
Cybersecurity Training and Certification
https://www.sans.org/

SHRM
Benefits of Employee Training Done Right
https://www.shrm.org/topics-tools/news/

Stickman Cyber
Why Cybersecurity in the Workplace is Everybody's Responsibility
https://www.stickmancyber.com/cybersecurity-blog/why-cybersecurity-in-the-workplace-is-everyones-responsibility

TechTarget Network
Cybersecurity Skills Gap
https://www.techtarget.com/searchsecurity/tip/Cybersecurity-skills-gap-Why-it-exists-and-how-to-address-it

Trellix
Survey Findings: A Look at the Cyber Talent Gap
https://www.trellix.com/blogs/perspectives/trellix-survey-findings-a-closer-look-at-the-cyber-talent-gap/

University of San Diego
How Can I Get an Entry-Level Cybersecurity Job
https://onlinedegrees.sandiego.edu/entry-level-cyber-security-jobs-guide/

U.S. Bureau of Labor Statistics
Information Security Analyst Jobs
https://www.bls.gov/opub/mlr/2023/home.htm

U.S. Homeland Security
Cybersecurity Apprenticeship Program
https://www.dhs.gov/homeland-security-careers/cybersecurity-apprenticeship-program

U.S. Homeland Security
Cybersecurity Internship Program
https://www.dhs.gov/homeland-security-careers/cybersecurity-internship-program

U.S. Jobs
Apply for Cybersecurity Jobs with the Federal Government
https://www.usajobs.gov

WiCyS
Women in Cybersecurity
https://www.wicys.org/

White House
National Cyber Workforce and Education Strategy
https://www.whitehouse.gov/wp-content/uploads/2023/07/NCWES-2023.07.31.pdf

ABOUT THE AUTHOR

Edward Moskal is an Associate Professor and the Founding Director of the Master's in Cyber Security Program and Cyber Security Center at Saint Peter's University in Jersey City, New Jersey. He has been a faculty member at Saint Peter's University for twenty years. Prior to Saint Peter's, Ed's background includes 24 years of work in information technology, including eight years as a Senior Manager and the Application Controls Consulting and Security Practice Leader for Ernst & Young in New York City. Professor Moskal is also a U.S. Secret Service Partner (Cyber Operations) for the NY/NJ Electronic Crimes Task Force. His expertise is in cyber security, workforce development ecosystems, learning and employment records, and product development.

www.ingramcontent.com/pod-product-compliance
Lightning Source LLC
Chambersburg PA
CBHW040244220526
45473CB00001B/367